BOOK of SPACE
Questions and Answers

By Rosie McCormick

CELEBRATION PRESS
Pearson Learning Group

Contents

Introduction

What do you want to know about space?

People have always asked questions about space. You can find answers to some of your questions in this book. Scientists have found many answers to their questions by using telescopes, spacecraft, and other tools. They have made amazing discoveries, but there is still much more to explore.

Space

What makes up space?

When you look up at the night sky, you are looking at space. Space is filled with many things, including planets, moons, stars, and other objects. A star is a ball of gas that gives off light and heat. A planet is a large object that moves around a star. A moon is an object that moves around a planet.

What is our place in space?

We live on a planet called Earth. Earth moves around the Sun, which is a star. Many objects move around the Sun, including nine major planets. Earth is the third planet from the Sun.

Earth

Stars

What makes the stars shine?

Stars are huge balls of gas. They produce heat and light. Most stars look like bright dots because they are so far away. We cannot see their real colors. Very hot stars are blue. Medium-hot stars are yellow. The coolest stars are red.

The brightness of a star depends on how much light it produces. The hotter a star is, the more brightly it shines. Large stars are usually brighter than small stars. The closer a star is to Earth, the brighter it appears to us.

hot stars

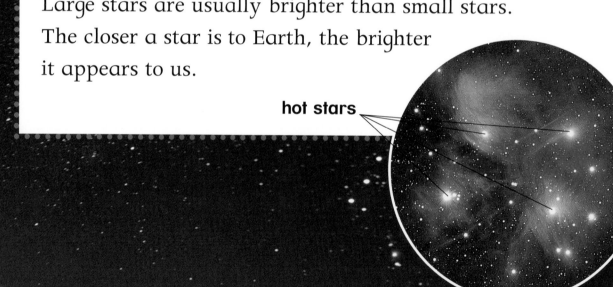

Why do we only see most stars at night?

The Sun is the closest star to Earth. It is so close that it appears very bright. During the day the Sun is so bright that we usually cannot see other stars. Even though we cannot see the other stars and planets during the daytime, they are still in space.

What are constellations?

Sometimes people imagine that the stars form pictures in the sky. Sometimes they see the shapes of animals, objects, and people. Constellations are the groups of stars that form these pictures. Long ago some people gave the star pictures names such as the Lion, the Scorpion, and the Southern Cross. There are eighty-eight constellations that we can see in the entire sky.

Scorpion

Southern Cross

Lion

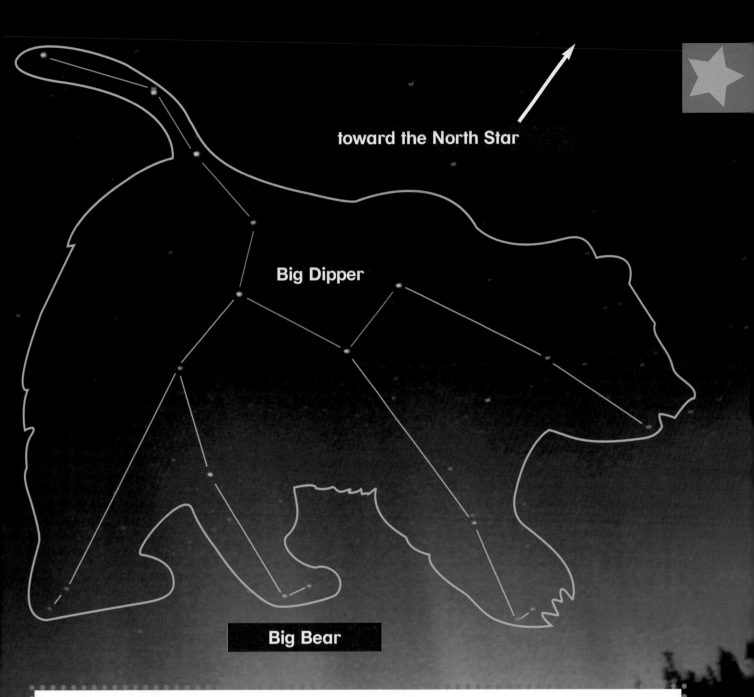

toward the North Star

Big Dipper

Big Bear

How do star watchers use constellations?

Star gazers use constellations to find individual stars. For example, one constellation is called the Big Bear. It contains a smaller group of seven stars called the Big Dipper. Two bright stars in the Big Dipper help you find the North Star. Sometimes when people are lost, they use the North Star to guide them.

The Sun

What kind of star is the Sun?

The Sun is a yellow star. The temperature of the center of the Sun is more than 25 million degrees Fahrenheit. For a star, that is only medium-hot. The Sun is much bigger than Earth. More than a million Earths could fit inside our Sun. Compared to other stars, however, the Sun is medium-sized.

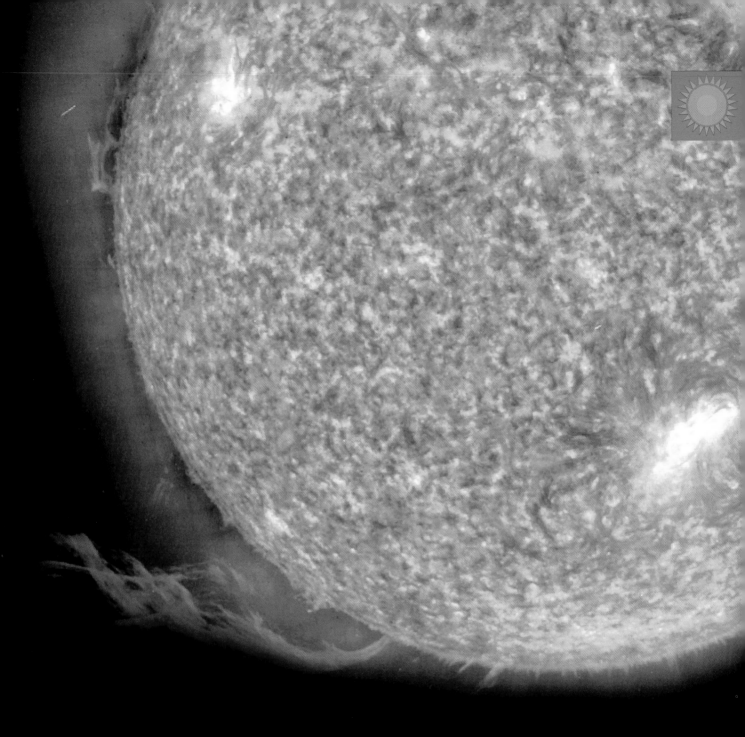

How far away is the Sun?

The Sun is about 93 million miles from Earth. If Earth were closer to the Sun, it would be too hot for people to live on our planet. If it were much farther away, it would be too cold.

The Moon

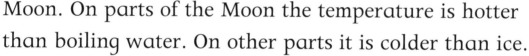

What is it like on the Moon?

The Moon is an object that moves around Earth. Like Earth, the Moon has rocks and soil. The surface of the Moon has many holes. These holes are called craters. There are also mountains on the Moon. On parts of the Moon the temperature is hotter than boiling water. On other parts it is colder than ice.

Can people live on the Moon?

People cannot live on the Moon today. Plants and animals need air to breathe and water to drink. There is no air or water on the Moon. To live on the Moon, people must bring air and water with them.

The craters on the Moon vary in size from less than an inch to many miles across.

How far away is the Moon?

The Moon is about 238,000 miles from Earth. If you could drive to the Moon, it would take months to get there. If you traveled by a spacecraft, it would take a few days. The Moon is our closest neighbor in space.

Moon

Earth

How does the Moon shine?

Even though the Moon shines, it has no light of its own. The light from the Moon comes from the Sun. The Sun shines on the Moon just like it shines on Earth. People see the part of the Moon that has the Sun's light shining on it.

light

Sun

Moon

light

Earth

Why does the Moon seem to change shape?

The Moon travels around Earth. As the Moon moves, only the surface that is lighted by the Sun can be seen on Earth. This makes it look like the Moon changes shape. The Moon does not change shape. It is always a sphere, like the shape of a ball.

full Moon

quarter Moon

crescent Moon

Our Solar System

What is our solar system?

Our solar system is made up of the Sun and the objects that move around it. There are nine major planets in our solar system. Many of them have moons. There are more than one hundred moons in all. There are also millions of smaller objects in our solar system such as asteroids and comets. Scientists discover new objects in our solar system all the time.

comet

What is an orbit?

An orbit is the path an object takes when it travels around something. When we say a planet "orbits" the Sun, we mean it follows a path around the Sun. All the planets in our solar system orbit the Sun. The Moon orbits Earth. Other moons orbit other planets.

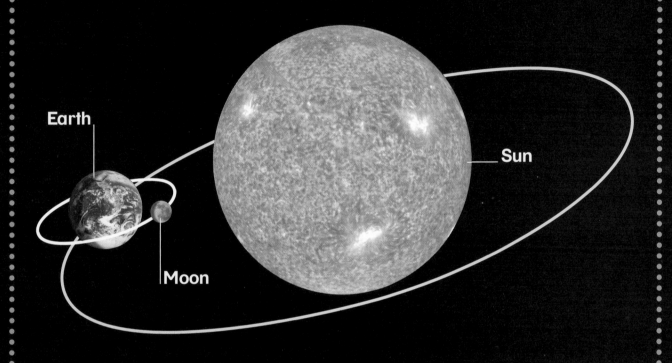

Earth

Sun

Moon

asteroid

What are the planets in our solar system?

The nine major planets in our solar system are Mercury, Venus, Earth, Mars, Jupiter, Saturn, Uranus, Neptune, and Pluto. Pluto is the smallest and Jupiter is the biggest of these planets.

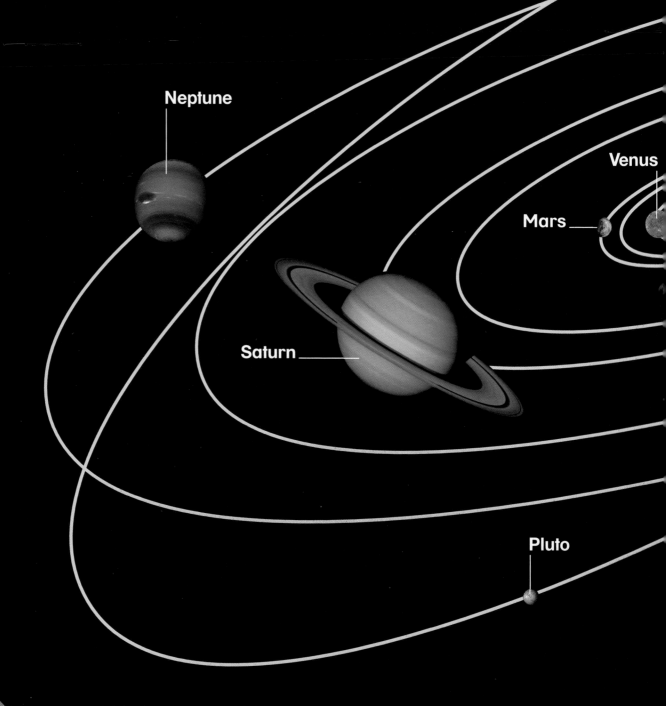

Neptune

Venus

Mars

Saturn

Pluto

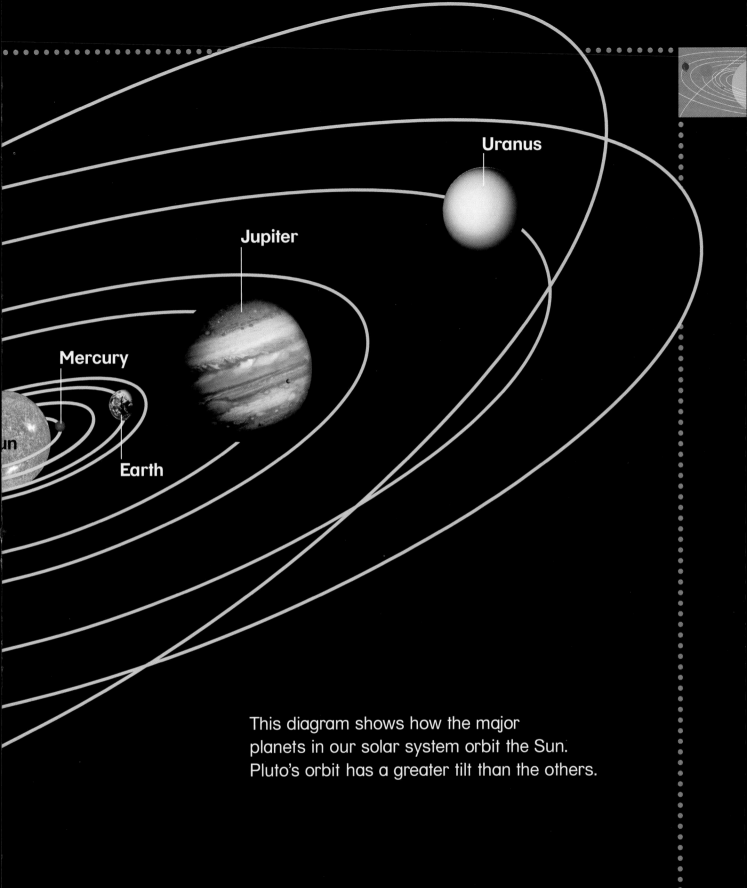

Uranus

Jupiter

Mercury

Sun

Earth

This diagram shows how the major
planets in our solar system orbit the Sun.
Pluto's orbit has a greater tilt than the others.

Exploring Space

How do people explore space?

Long ago people explored space by looking at the night sky. Today scientists still do this, but they use telescopes to help them see more clearly. Astronauts and machines called space probes also explore space.

These telescopes on Mauna Kea, Hawaii, take pictures of space objects.

What do telescopes do?

People use telescopes to study space. Telescopes make distant objects appear larger and brighter. They allow people to see far into space more clearly. Some telescopes are used to take pictures of planets and stars.

Today scientists use computers to control most telescopes. Some telescopes are on Earth. Others, like the Hubble Space Telescope, are in space.

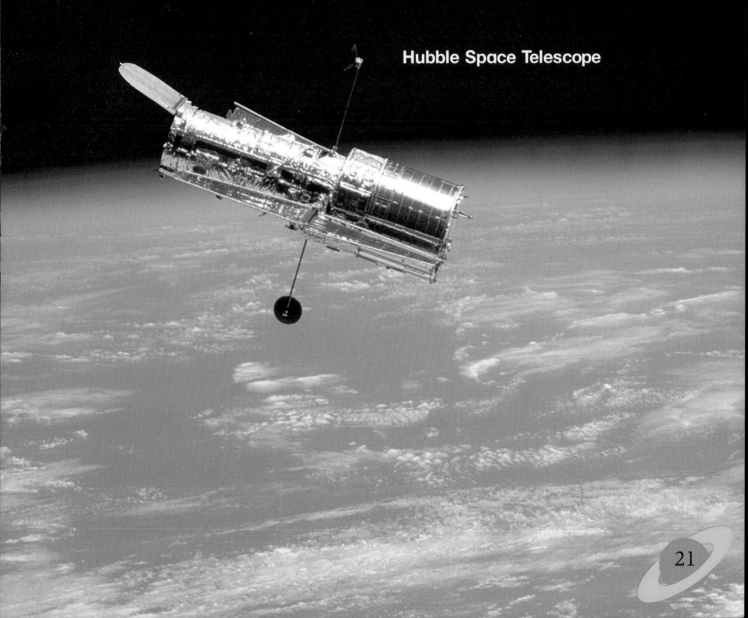

Hubble Space Telescope

What are space probes?

Space probes are machines that study space. The machines go to faraway planets and moons. Probes collect information and take close-up pictures that a telescope on Earth could not take.

One space probe scientists have used is called *Galileo*. The space probe took pictures of volcanoes erupting on one of Jupiter's moons. It sent the information and pictures back to scientists on Earth.

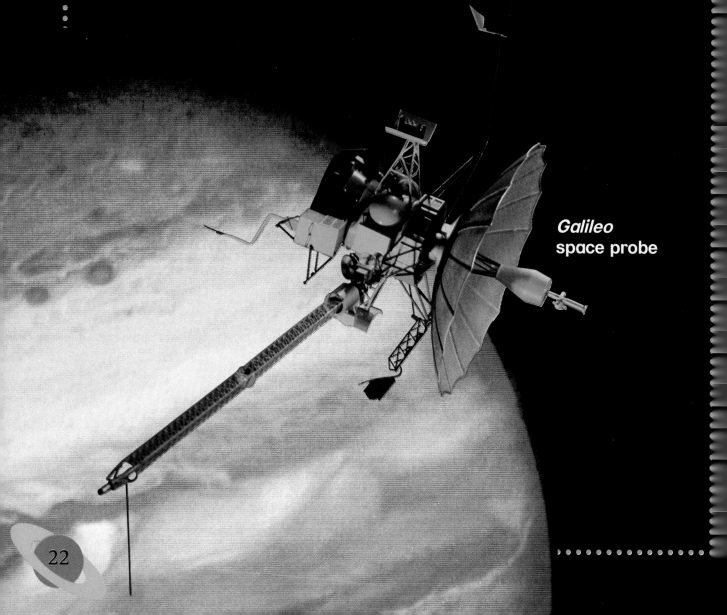

Galileo
space probe

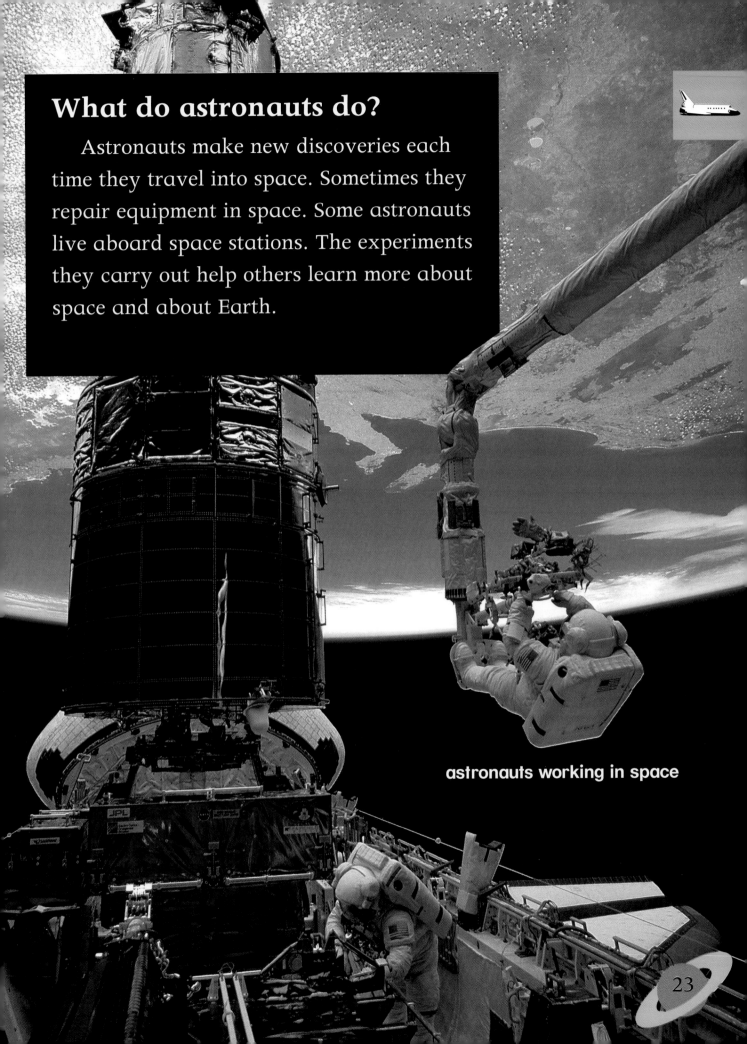

What do astronauts do?

Astronauts make new discoveries each time they travel into space. Sometimes they repair equipment in space. Some astronauts live aboard space stations. The experiments they carry out help others learn more about space and about Earth.

astronauts working in space

Key Events in Space Exploration

1957 *Sputnik I* is launched. It is the first object made by humans to orbit the Earth.

1959 *Luna 2* is the first spacecraft to land on the Moon.

1961 Cosmonaut Yuri Gagarin is the first person to travel in space. He journeys once around Earth on April 12, in a flight lasting 108 minutes.

1968 *Apollo 8* is the first spacecraft to fly with people around the Moon and return to Earth.

1969 On the *Apollo 11* mission, astronaut Neil Armstrong is the first person to walk on the Moon on July 20.

1981 The Space Shuttle *Columbia* is sent into orbit around Earth. It is the first spacecraft that could be reused in space.

1990 The Space Shuttle *Discovery* releases the Hubble Space Telescope. Its purpose is to study objects in space.

2000 The International Space Station opens in November. Astronauts and scientists from many nations live and work on the space station. They study what it is like to live in space.